Janet Stone
and John Willis

www.av2books.com

Step 1
Go to **www.av2books.com**

Step 2
Enter this unique code
KNREHGBQ9

Step 3
Explore your interactive eBook!

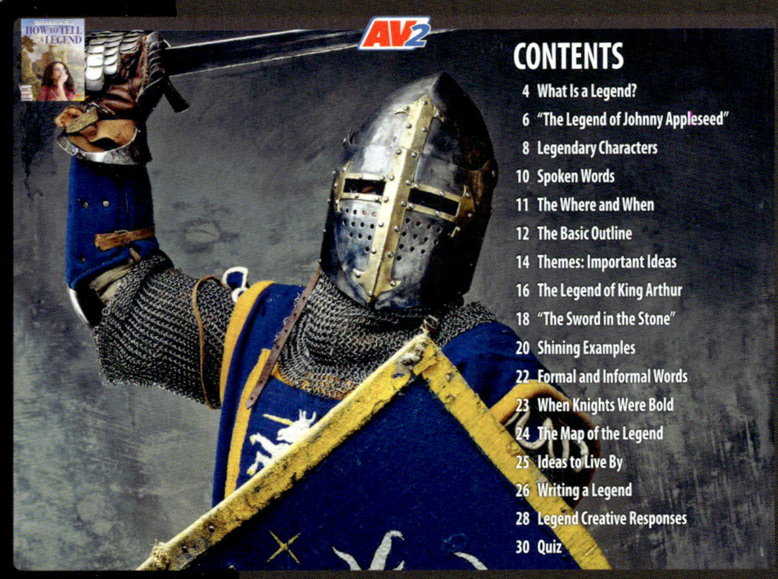

AV2 is optimized for use on any device

Your interactive eBook comes with...

Contents
Browse a live contents page to easily navigate through resources

Audio
Listen to sections of the book read aloud

Videos
Watch informative video clips

Weblinks
Gain additional information for research

Try This!
Complete activities and hands-on experiments

Key Words
Study vocabulary, and complete a matching word activity

Quizzes
Test your knowledge

Slideshows
View images and captions

... and much, much more!

Contents

What Is a Legend?

Johnny Appleseed, King Arthur, and Robin Hood— do these people sound familiar? They are all **heroes** from stories called **legends**. A legend is a story from long ago that has been passed down from generation to generation. Most legends tell the story of a hero who performs great **feats** or good deeds. Legends are often based on a real person or **event** from history. Over time, as the legend is retold, some details get changed or exaggerated.

Many people have tried to prove that Robin Hood was a historical figure, but no one has succeeded so far.

The first legends are thousands of years old. They began as spoken stories told to one person and passed to another. These stories were later written down. Examples of legends can be found in every culture. In some legends, the hero is a national or **folk hero**.

Legends are usually exciting and entertaining stories about heroes and their adventures. Legends can also teach people about the culture they come from. These legends inspire people around the world.

Write Your Own Legend

1 Prewriting

Think of a legend you might want to write. Follow each step as you read through this book to help create a legend of your own.

A legend begins with a hero. Who will your hero be? Write down **characters** you can use as the hero of your legend. Think of a character who is strong and brave. Or, start with a character who might become a hero by doing a great deed.

The Legend of Johnny Appleseed

John Chapman was born in Leominster, Massachusetts, in 1774. Johnny and his family lived on a farm. The family farm had good soil for growing crops. In the spring, bees buzzed around the sweet-smelling apple blossoms. Sometimes, Johnny would climb up a tree to a beehive to get a taste of the bees' honey.

"Thank you for sharing your honey. I won't disturb you any longer," he would tell the bees. Johnny knew that bees worked hard for their honey. He never took more than a taste.

Johnny sure did like apples, too. They were about the only sweet thing people had to eat in those days.

But as good as life was in Massachusetts, Johnny thought it was too proper. He liked being outdoors in the forests.

Johnny grew restless, and when he was a young man, he set out to explore the lands to the west. He carried with him a big bag of apple seeds that he'd received from a cider mill.

Johnny was an odd kind of fellow. He hiked up and down the hills wearing old worn-out shoes. He had to stuff the holes with leaves and hold them together with string and rags! Why, some folks didn't know what to make of him. But Johnny was friendly to the people he met, and they welcomed him into their homes. He made sleds and wagons for their children and gave bits of ribbon to the little girls.

Whenever he came to settlers' farms, he told them, "You need to plant apple trees. Apples make good eating when you pick them off a tree. You can dry them and eat them all winter long. You can make tasty apple butter and apple cider." And then he would give them some seeds to plant in their fields.

Sometimes, he sold seeds or traded them for clothes. Usually, he gave the seeds away. After all, Johnny didn't need much. He lived alone in the woods and walked most everywhere he wanted to go. People saw him walking by dressed in old, raggedy clothes and wearing a pot for a hat!

Soon, the Ohio Valley had many apple orchards that John had planted. He took good care of them, too. But Johnny soon grew restless again. He piled bags of apple seeds into a canoe and set out for Indiana. Just as he had done in Ohio, he gave his seeds to the settlers he met. "Plant these seeds," he told them. "These seeds will grow into fine apple trees. Apples will feed you all winter long!"

Pretty soon, people began telling stories about this odd man. They started calling him Johnny Appleseed.

Many settlers shared their stories about Johnny. "Johnny cares about others, for sure. One winter a man gave Johnny some boots," said one settler. "The next time Johnny passed by, he was barefoot. The man asked what happened to the boots. Johnny said that he gave the boots away to someone who needed them more."

Said another settler, "I heard that one winter Johnny was fixin' to sleep in a cave to get out of the snow. But a bear and her cubs were already sleeping there. So Johnny says to the bear, 'I reckon I'll just have to find another place to sleep, seein' as how this cave belongs to you.' "

When Johnny was 71 years old, he got news that some cattle had broken into an apple orchard. Off he went to protect it. Sadly, his old, thin body could not take the long journey and Johnny died. To honor his memory, he was buried near one of his apple orchards.

Legendary Characters

A legend is based on a real person who lived during a particular time and place. The main character in a legend is always a hero. This hero has qualities that we admire. These qualities are called traits. A trait is part of a hero's personality that does not change. For example, a hero is usually confident. The hero may sometimes feel worried or scared, but most of the time, he or she acts boldly and confidently.

Heroes in a legend have a purpose, or mission. Johnny Appleseed wanted new settlers to plant apple trees so they would have food to eat. Johnny believed in his cause. He was honest and hard-working. He showed determination. These character traits help us understand him.

The real Johnny Appleseed, a man named John Chapman, lived in the American Midwest between 1774 and 1845.

"The Legend of Johnny Appleseed" tells the story of an ordinary person who did extraordinary things. We learn about Johnny's traits through his actions. We can also learn about Johnny by paying close attention to descriptions and details in the story. The passage below, from another story, describes a small moment in Johnny Appleseed's life.

About noontime, Johnny's stomach rumbled with hunger. He pulled some cornbread and a handful of nuts from his sack. As he bit into his cornbread, a squirrel hopped close. Johnny chuckled softly and held out a handful of nuts. "All creatures under the sky got to eat," he said.

Pay close attention to the descriptions and details. We know that Johnny is kind to animals and living things. He is generous and shares what little he has.

European settlers learned how to make cornbread from Native Americans.

Write Your Own Legend

2 Explore Your Hero

What makes your character special? Is your character smart and clever? Will he or she need to use cleverness and a quick mind to solve a problem or do something special? Or does your character rely on courage and strength? Heroes in legends are "larger than life." Exaggerate the character's traits.

Spoken Words

The words that characters speak in a legend are called **dialogue**. Dialogue makes characters seem like real people and helps the story come alive. We can learn a lot about characters by what they say and how they say it. Read this dialogue out loud. Can you hear Johnny's gentleness?

"Thank you for sharing your honey. I won't disturb you any longer."

Dialect is a particular way of speaking. Some people use different grammar and say words in a different way. Johnny pronounces words differently in the settler's story. Instead of saying "seeing," he drops the letter "g" at the end of the word. "I reckon" is a way of saying "I suppose" or "I think." Johnny Appleseed would not say, "I see that this cave belongs to you." He would say "seein' as how." These word choices are important in painting a picture of a character.

Think About It!

Imagine that Johnny Appleseed was making a sled for a boy or giving ribbons to a girl. Write a conversation between Johnny and the child. Make the dialogue sound realistic by using dialect.

The Where and When

A legend takes place in a particular time and place. This time and place is the **setting**. The people who first told the legend wanted to honor someone who was important to their history and culture. "The Legend of Johnny Appleseed" takes place in the early 1800s. Most of the story takes place in the Ohio Valley. Details help readers picture the time and place.

But John was friendly to the people he met, and they welcomed him into their homes. He made sleds and wagons for their children and gave bits of ribbon to the little girls.

What does this passage teach us about the time and place?

- In the 1800s, people passing by a farm were welcomed, since they often brought news.
- Most people walked to get around.
- Many wore old clothes.
- Children were happy to get a sled or some ribbons.

These small details help readers understand why the characters act, talk, and dress the way they do.

Although designs have changed greatly since the 1800s, sledding is still a popular pastime today.

The Basic Outline

A legend begins with a problem. The events show how the hero solves the problem. The turning point, or **climax**, comes when the hero solves the problem. The turning point is the most exciting part. After the climax, the events are neatly wrapped up in a satisfying way. This part of the legend is called the **resolution**.

Legends often have positive and inspiring endings. The hero usually succeeds in doing what he or she sets out to do. "The Legend of Johnny Appleseed" follows his life, from his birth to his death. It has a beginning, middle, and end.

Over time, people added many tales to Johnny Appleseed's story. One of these tales was set during the War of 1812 between the United States and Great Britain. Villages in the Ohio territory were being attacked. When a town near him was attacked, Johnny Appleseed ran through the night in bare feet to warn settlers and get help.

Write Your Own Legend

3 Problems! Problems!

A good hero needs something to fight or a problem to solve. Start with a good problem for your hero to face. Does your hero have to rescue someone? Does he or she have to deliver an important message? How will your character solve this problem? Write the main events. One event may lead you to another. Let your ideas flow!

Story Map for "Johnny Appleseed Went Barefoot"

A **story map** shows the basic parts of a **plot**.

Characters

Johnny Appleseed, soldiers, settlers

Setting

The War of 1812

Problem

Johnny needs to get help.

Events

1. Settlers learn they may be attacked.
2. They gather together in a lookout building for safety.
3. Johnny runs all night to a fort to get help.
4. Climax: Johnny makes it to the fort at sunrise and tells soldiers to come and protect the settlers.
5. Soldiers march to the lookout building to protect the settlers.
6. Settlers go home.

Resolution

The settlers tell the story about how Johnny ran for help. The story spreads and becomes part of the legend.

Themes: Important Ideas

Legends have heroes we admire. Everybody values people who are brave, kind, and act with honor. We create legends about people who made a sacrifice or gave up something to help others. Heroes in legends have qualities we value in our culture.

Legends are based on big ideas, or **themes**, that teach us lessons about life. The lesson can often be stated in short phrases. For example:

- Love is stronger than hate.
- Forgiving others will set you free.
- Follow your dreams.

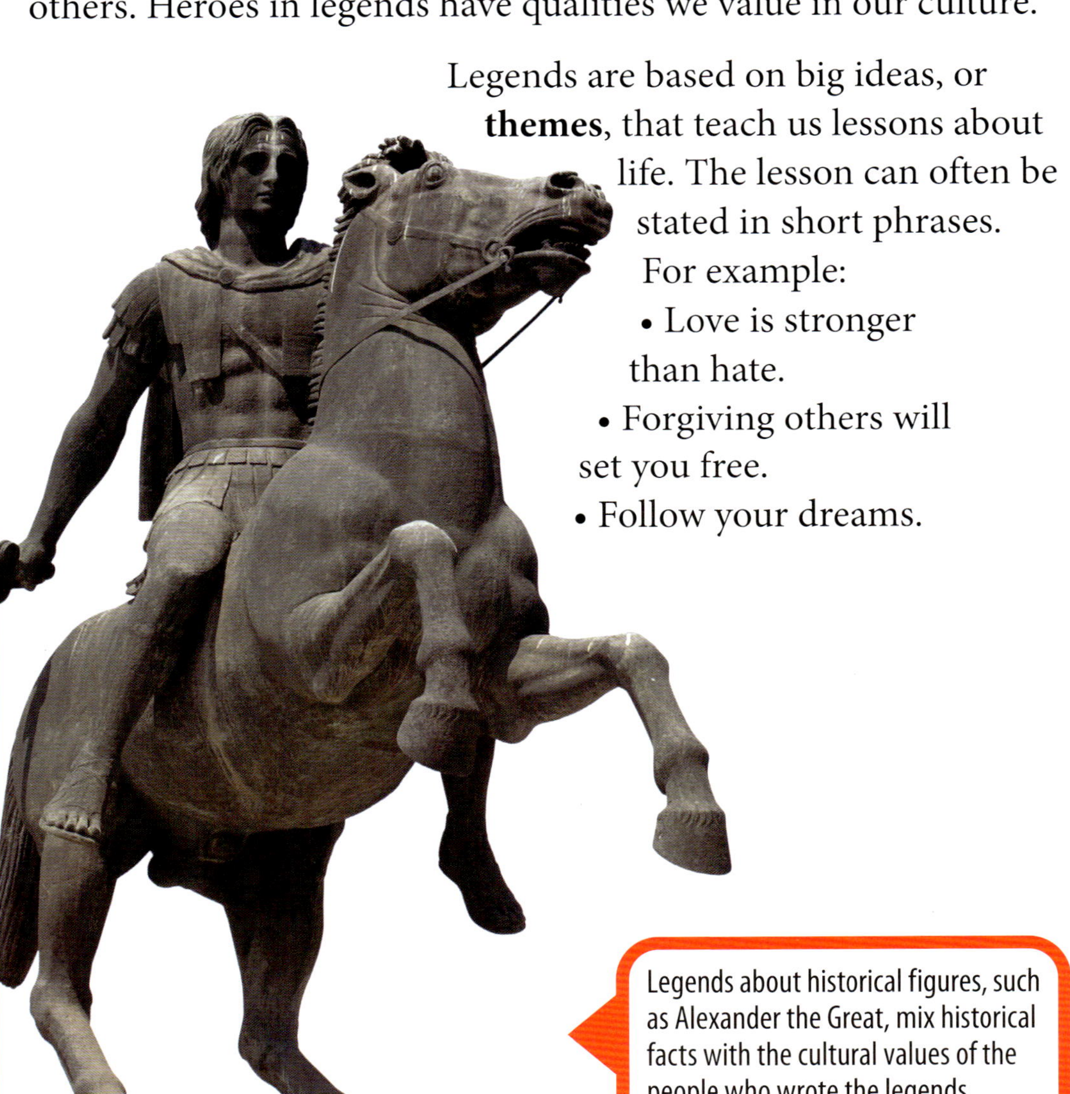

Legends about historical figures, such as Alexander the Great, mix historical facts with the cultural values of the people who wrote the legends.

Many of the themes found in ancient legends are used today in tales such as superhero stories.

Think About It!

Choose a favorite legend. What theme or themes can you find in it? Write the theme and explain why it is important. What life lesson does it teach?

The Legend of King Arthur

The legend of King Arthur is based on a person who may have lived in England hundreds of years ago. The legend grew about the king's many accomplishments. King Arthur and his knights performed brave acts. It was said they rescued maidens and fought dragons. King Arthur united the people of England and brought peace to the land.

Today, stories about King Arthur have affected how many people think of England during the Middle Ages.

The legend of King Arthur begins at his birth. Arthur was the son of King Uther. When Arthur was born, his father was afraid that his enemies would harm his son. He asked Merlin, a wise magician, to watch over Arthur. Merlin took Arthur away to a man named Sir Ector, who raised Arthur as though he was his own son. Arthur would not be told that his real father was King Uther until the time was right. In "The Sword in the Stone," Arthur discovers his true identity.

Write Your Own Legend

4 Write a First Draft

Write your first draft. Do not worry about making mistakes. Just get your ideas down on paper and use your notes. Include the key events in a story map. But if your ideas take you in a different direction, follow them! The best ideas will come while you are writing.

Things to Keep in Mind:

- Why did people tell stories about your hero?
- What great deed did your hero do?
- What kind of dialogue would your hero speak?
- What details will help make your hero seem real to the reader?

The Sword in the Stone

Merlin, a wise magician, called all men of noble birth in England to come to London to participate in a **jousting** tournament. King Uther had died in battle, leaving England in need of a leader. The winner of the tournament would be crowned king.

When Sir Ector heard this news, he called his son, Sir Kay, and Arthur to his side. "Kay, you have trained well and hard to be a knight. I bid you come with me to London and enter the jousting tournament. You will bring honor to our family." He turned to face Arthur, who had served Sir Kay for the past years. "Arthur, you are to stay at Kay's side and assist him in the tournament."

Arthur stood tall. His heart swelled. "I will be proud to carry Sir Kay's sword and flag."

The day of the jousting tournament was bright and clear. Flags fluttered in the breeze. The benches were filled with lords and ladies dressed in richly colored robes. The knights' armor shone in the sunlight. Arthur gazed with wonder at the scene. Never had he seen such a noble sight!

As Arthur led Sir Kay in his armor toward his horse, Sir Kay drew his sword and swung it as though he was in battle. The sword hit metal and broke in two.

Sir Kay cried out in horror, "Arthur, go quickly back to our tents and get my father's sword!"

"I will go with all speed!" And off Arthur ran as fast as he could.

As he ran, he thought of a sword that he had seen in the cathedral square. This sword was stuck in a stone. "Surely it will be faster to pull that sword out of the stone than to run all the way back to our tents," he thought. "I will not let Kay down. He must have a sword at once."

Arthur ran to the square and grabbed the sword. It came out smoothly and easily. A thrill went through him. He looked upon it with wide eyes, then shook himself awake. "Make haste!" he said to himself, and off he ran to Sir Kay.

"I have your sword," he panted.

When Sir Kay saw it, his face turned white. "Where did you get this sword?" he asked in a strange voice.

"I pulled it out from the stone," replied Arthur.

Sir Kay paused. How he longed to own the sword! But he kneeled before Arthur. "My lord, I am your servant."

"Nay, arise, Kay," said Arthur.

"The sword you hold is special. Hundreds of men before you have tried to free it from the stone. Look closely at the sword and you will understand."

Arthur looked at the handle and read aloud in wonder, "Whoever pulls this sword from the stone is the rightful king of England."

Sir Ector and Merlin approached. "Aye, Merlin brought you to me as a baby, away from those who might harm you. Your father was King Uther. Merlin told me to watch over you until the time was right."

Merlin then called everyone to the square. He commanded Arthur to put the sword back in the stone and pull it out for all to see. Once, twice, three times Arthur drew the sword from the stone.

"Behold your king, Arthur, the son of King Uther!" cried Merlin.

A hush fell over the crowd, then cheers rang out. "Long live the king!" they cried.

Arthur had fulfilled his destiny to become king, and his heart lifted with joy and gladness.

Shining Examples

Heroes in legends are loyal and brave. When you read a legend, pay close attention to details. In "The Sword in the Stone," Arthur's actions provide clues about his character. Read these sentences from the story.

Arthur stood tall. His heart swelled. "I will be proud to carry Sir Kay's sword and flag."

Based on these sentences, readers can figure out that Arthur is a good and loyal person.

Arthur is the main character in the legend. Sir Kay is a minor character. Minor characters are not at the center of the legend. However, they give the main character a chance to speak and act. They can be important in moving the plot forward.

Write Your Own Legend

5 Revise Your Legend

Read your legend aloud. Find parts that can be improved.

Things to Keep in Mind:

- Does it have details about the time and place?
- Does it have dialogue?
- Does it have actions that show what the hero is like?

The main characters in legends are often royalty or nobility. Charlemagne, an 8th-century French king, was the subject of many legends.

Formal and Informal Words

Dialogue tells the reader what a character is thinking and feeling. It can also be used to move the action of the legend forward.

In "The Legend of Johnny Appleseed," characters spoke in dialect. They sounded the way people spoke in everyday life. In this legend, the dialogue is formal. When Sir Ector says, "I bid you come with me," he is using formal language. He is telling Sir Kay to come with him to London.

The dialogue in the legend of "The Sword in the Stone" helps to create a serious tone, or mood. The dialogue in "The Legend of Johnny Appleseed" is less formal than the dialogue in "The Sword in the Stone." The less formal dialogue creates a lighthearted tone.

Write Your Own Legend

6 Proofread Your Draft

Now reread your legend. Fix any mistakes.

Things to Keep in Mind:

- Did you use quotation marks around dialogue?
- Did you use capital letters for the names?
- Did you spell all words correctly?

When Knights Were Bold

The legend of "The Sword in the Stone" is set in England in the Middle Ages. This setting is a time and place that stirs our imagination.

Arthur most likely lived around 600 AD in England. Life was hard in the Middle Ages. Castles were cold and dark, and many people were poor and hungry. Most legends do not include these things in the setting. Instead, the legend makes life in early England seem exciting and full of adventure.

Authors use descriptions to make the setting seem real. Then, readers use their own imaginations to add more details.

Camelot, King Arthur's palace, is the setting of many legends. The location itself was likely fictional.

Think About It!

Reading legends can help people learn about history. Draw a picture of a tournament. Include knights on horseback. Use details from this legend and the illustrations. Find out more by reading other books about the Middle Ages.

The Map of the Legend

The plot in "The Sword in the Stone" features common characteristics found in most legends. The first part of the story introduces us to the characters and the setting. Sir Kay and Arthur travel to London for the jousting tournament. Then, the problem is introduced. Sir Kay breaks his sword. Arthur must get him a new one. This shows how minor characters, such as Sir Kay, play an important part in the plot.

Swords were first invented about 5,000 years ago.

Story Map for "The Sword in the Stone"

Characters
Arthur, Merlin, Sir Ector, Sir Kay

Setting
England in the Middle Ages

Resolution
Arthur fulfills his destiny to become king.

Ideas to Live By

The themes of truth and honor are at the heart of many legends. Knights in legends fight for truth and honor, and follow a code of honor.

The themes in the legend of "The Sword in the Stone" teach lessons including "rise to a challenge," "act with loyalty," and "be honest."

Write Your Own Legend

7 Make a Final Copy

Copy your legend neatly on a new piece of paper. Add a title. Think of ways to share your writing. You could make a cover for your story. You may want to draw a picture that has details about the setting. You can also read your legend aloud to your family and friends.

Problem

Sir Kay needs a sword.

Events

1. Arthur goes to find a sword.
2. He takes a sword from a stone.
3. Arthur gives the sword to Sir Kay.
4. Sir Kay kneels before Arthur. He calls Arthur "my lord."
5. Climax: Arthur learns that he is a king.

Writing a Legend

Writing a legend may take several tries. It is important to look over each draft of a story you write. You may find things that are wrong or that you wish to change.

Hector decided to write about Davy Crockett. His first draft is short because he is just getting started. He has included his main character, the problem, some main events, and a possible solution.

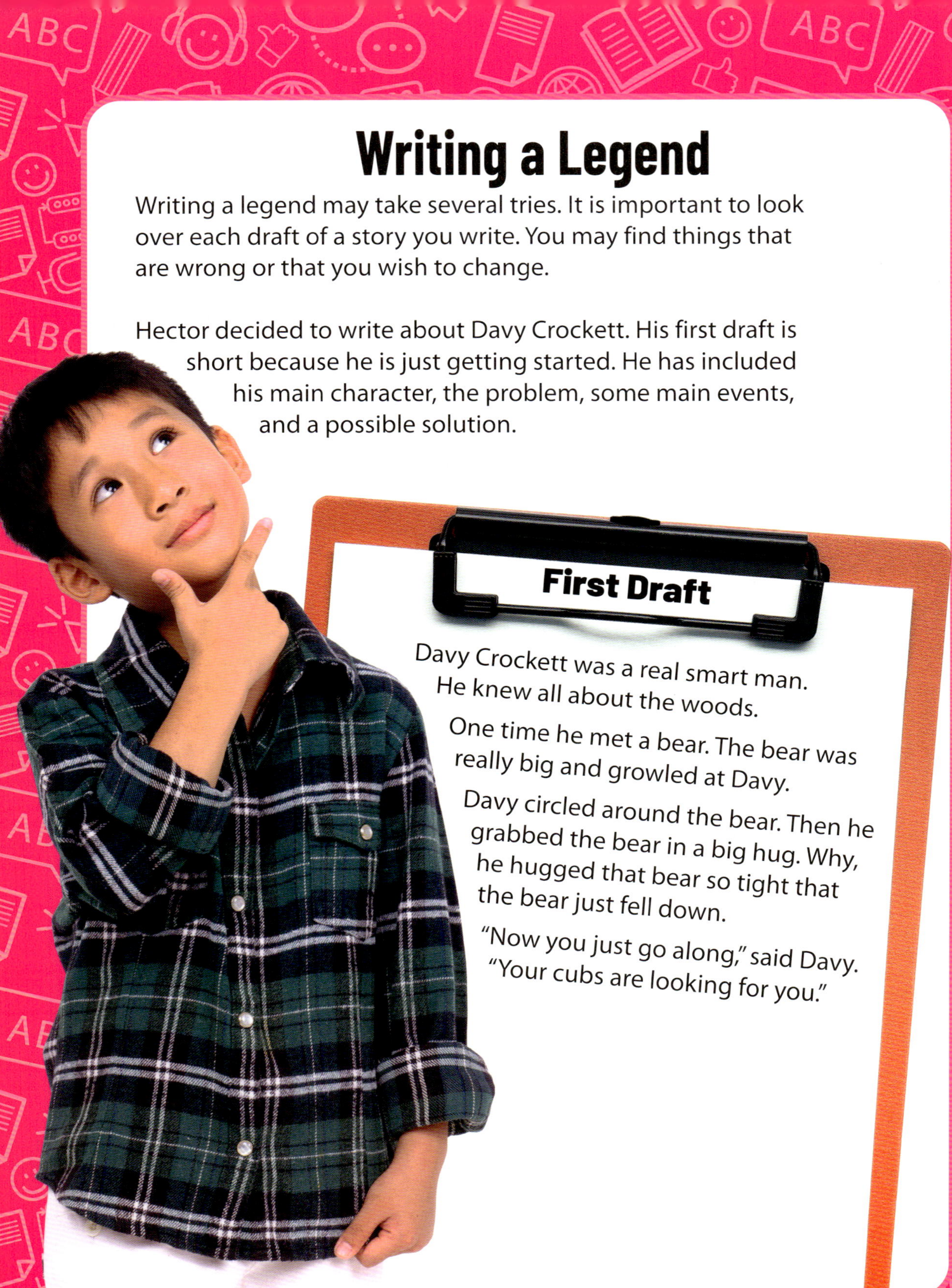

First Draft

Davy Crockett was a real smart man. He knew all about the woods.

One time he met a bear. The bear was really big and growled at Davy.

Davy circled around the bear. Then he grabbed the bear in a big hug. Why, he hugged that bear so tight that the bear just fell down.

"Now you just go along," said Davy. "Your cubs are looking for you."

Proofreading Symbols

Use the symbols below when looking through your first draft of a story.

delete	replace	make upper case	insert
bearrs	~~foxes~~ squirrels	davy Crockett	a big hug

Hector continued to work on his legend. He added some descriptive details about Davy. He also added details about the setting.

Second Draft

Davy Crockett was a real smart man. He knew all about the woods. He didn't have to go to school to learn everything there was to know.

One time, he was out cutting a trail in the Tennessee woods. All of a sudden, he met a bear. That bear was twice as tall as Davy. It growled at Davy.

Davy acted like he wasn't scared. "Howdy, bear," said Davy. "There's no need for you to get so mad. I ain't goin' to harm you."

Davy grabbed the bear in a big hug. The bear fell down. Davy and that bear rolled down the trail and back up again. Davy hugged that bear until the bear got tired.

"Whew!" said Davy. "What a big bear hug!" And from that time on, everybody knew that Davy was going to be the king of the wild frontier.

Legend Creative Responses

Now you know what a legend is. Use what you learned to have fun with these creative activities. Share them with friends and classmates and compare your creations.

You Are There

Imagine that you were at the site of the climax of your favorite legend. Write a diary entry. Include details about the setting and the action. Make the moment come alive. How did you feel? Did you cheer?

Create a Poster

Create a poster to encourage people to follow a behavior or ideal from your favorite legend. Use reasons from the legend. Add your own persuasive reasons and write a catchy title. Include drawings in your poster.

Adding On

Add to the legend of your choice. Write a story about what you think happens after the resolution.

- Write dialogue that is similar to the way people spoke during the time of your legend's setting.
- Use descriptive details. Help the reader picture the setting, characters, and action.
- Use exaggeration. When something is exaggerated, we say that it is larger than life. This means it is bigger, or more extreme.

Journal Entry

Write a personal response about your favorite legend.

- What do you think of the characters in the legend?
- What qualities of these characters do you admire? Do they have qualities that you see in yourself?

Quiz

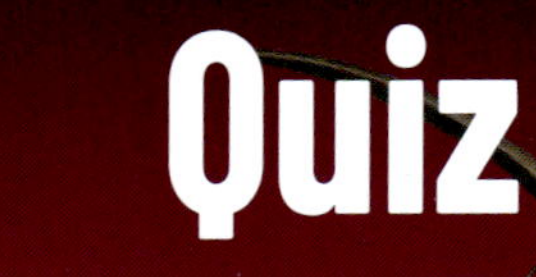

1 Is Sir Kay a minor character?

2 What was the real Johnny Appleseed's name?

3 What is the resolution of "The Sword in the Stone"?

4 What kinds of endings do legends often have?

5 How old are the first legends?

6 What is dialect?

7 When does "The Legend of Johnny Appleseed" take place?

8 Was Camelot a real location?

ANSWERS: 1 Yes 2 John Chapman 3 Arthur fulfills his destiny to become king. 4 Positive and inspiring 5 Thousands of years old 6 A particular way of speaking 7 The early 1800s 8 Probably not

Key Words

characters: the people, animals, or creatures in a story

climax: the peak of a story

dialect: the way people of a particular region speak

dialogue: the words that a character speaks

event: action that happens in a story

feats: acts of great courage or skill

folk hero: someone who is admired for their achievements by the people in a particular place

heroes: the most important characters in a legend

jousting: a sporting event in which knights on horseback charge at each other carrying large poles and try to knock each other off their horses

legends: stories about people who lived in a particular time and place

plot: the chain of events in a story

resolution: the end of the story, when the plot's main problem is solved

setting: the time and place in which a story takes place

story map: a diagram that shows the basic parts of a plot

themes: the main ideas or lessons in stories

Index

Get the best of both worlds.

AV2 bridges the gap between print and digital.

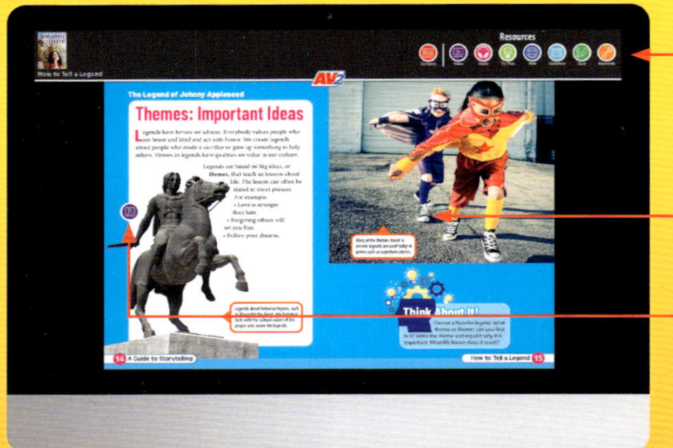

The expandable resources toolbar enables quick access to content including **videos**, **audio**, **activities**, **weblinks**, **slideshows**, **quizzes**, and **key words**.

Animated videos make static images come alive.

Resource icons on each page help readers to further **explore key concepts**.

Published by AV2
14 Penn Plaza, 9th Floor
New York, NY 10122
Website: www.av2books.com

Library of Congress Control Number: 2020935556

ISBN 978-1-7911-3151-7 (hardcover)
ISBN 978-1-7911-3152-4 (softcover)
ISBN 978-1-7911-3141-8 (multi-user eBook)
ISBN 978-1-7911-3153-1 (single-user eBook)

Printed in Guangzhou, China
1 2 3 4 5 6 7 8 9 0 24 23 22 21 20

072020
101319

Project Coordinator: John Willis
Designer: Ana María Vidal

Photo Credits
Every reasonable effort has been made to trace ownership and to obtain permission to reprint copyright material. The publisher would be pleased to have any errors or omissions brought to its attention so that they may be corrected in subsequent printings. AV2 acknowledges Getty Images, iStock, and Shutterstock as its primary image suppliers for this title.

First published by Crabtree Publishing Company in 2012.